THE
FLYING
MACHINE

A Stagecoach
Journey
in 1774

John J. Loeper

THE FLYING MACHINE

A Stagecoach Journey in 1774

ILLUSTRATED WITH OLD WOODCUTS

Atheneum 1976 New York

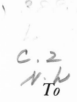

To

Rose, Catherine,
Stella, Alice, and Tess

Illustrations courtesy of the New York Public Library
Picture Collection

Library of Congress Cataloging in Publication Data
Loeper, John J.
The flying machine.
SUMMARY: *The experiences of a young boy travel-*
ing by stagecoach from Philadelphia to New York on
the Old York Road reveal the joys and discomforts
of this mode of transportation.
1. Coaching—United States—Juvenile literature.
[1. Coaching. 2. Carriages and carts] I. Title.
HE5623.L58   388.3'22'0974   75-13772
ISBN 0-689-30491-9

Contents

THE
FLYING
MACHINE

A Stagecoach
Journey
in 1774

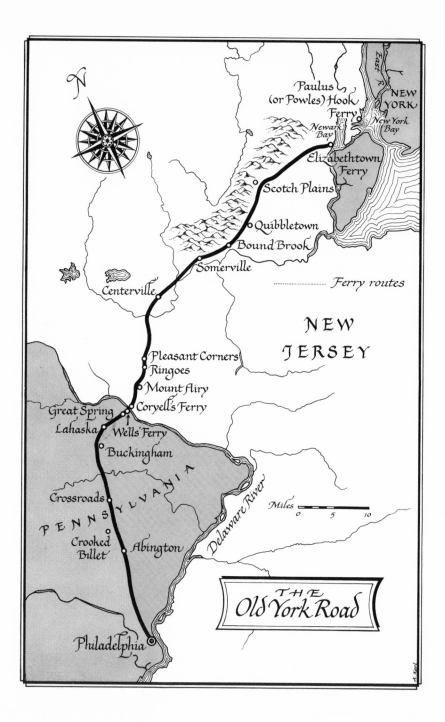

N

Paulus
(or Powles) Hook
Ferry

East R.

NEW
YORK

New York
Bay

Newark
Bay

Elizabethtown
Ferry

Scotch Plains

Quibbletown

Bound Brook

Somerville

Ferry routes

Centerville

NEW

JERSEY

Pleasant Corners
Ringoes
Mount Airy
Coryell's Ferry

Great Spring

Lahaska

Wells' Ferry

Buckingham

Crossroads

Delaware River

Miles

0   5   10

PENNSYLVANIA

Crooked
Billet

Abington

THE
Old York Road

Philadelphia

A. Korl

Preface

There is a story told that, on a moonlit night, the sound of a distant coach horn can be heard along the Old York Road. And some folks claim that a ghostly coach pulled by phantom horses rolls silently along the old highway in search of familiar landmarks.

Whether or not the story is true, the memory of stage-coach days lingers on along the Old York Road. Several of the inns that served the needs of early travelers are still in use, and ancient houses stand in quiet villages along the route. The road and its past are part of American history and heritage.

The Old York Road, now a series of concrete highways, blacktop roads, and city streets, was one of America's oldest highways. It joined Philadelphia and New York City and played an important role in the nation's history. It was used by the Continental Army during the Revolutionary War for the movement of men and supplies. It served in developing commerce between two large and important cities, and it was the main travel route across the state of New Jersey.

From the mid 1700s until the arrival of the railroads around 1840, stagecoaches served the York Road carrying mail and passengers. The advent of faster and more comfortable transportation put the stagecoach lines out of business. These lines were owned and operated by enterprising businessmen. Some were large, operating a fleet of coaches over the entire route. Others were quite small carrying passengers only a short distance between towns in a single coach.

One of the earliest and best known lines using the York Road was the Swift-Sure Stagecoach Line. Its coaches, called Flying Machines, traveled between Philadelphia and the ferries at Elizabethtown (Elizabeth) and Powles Hook (Jersey City) for over half a century.

Perhaps it is a ghostly Flying Machine that still haunts the old highway!

This is the story of a journey on a Flying Machine taken by a boy in 1774. The characters in the story are imaginary but the chronicle of the Old York Road and the Swift-Sure Stagecoach is fact. It is a story that might have been.

The 23rd of

1774

"Ca–at fish! Ca–at fish!"

The singsong cry of the fish vendor could be heard in the distance as ten-year-old David Wicks and his mother walked along the streets of old Philadelphia.

A "whitey-wash" man hurried by down Pewter-Platter Alley, on his way to whitewash the smoke-stained walls of some Philadelphia house.

And in Hutton's Lane, an old woman stood by a steaming soup kettle singing, "Peppery Pot, Steaming Hot! Peppery Pot, Steaming Hot!"

Although it was still early morning, the streets were crowded with people. In 1774, Philadelphia was the most important city in the colonies and the second largest city in the British Empire. It had over 40,000 residents.

Carriages clattered by on the cobblestones and wagons rumbled toward the docks. Carpenters, bricklayers, and other tradesmen strode along with their young apprentices tagging behind. Proper Quaker businessmen passed by in their drab clothing and wide-brimmed hats. And at the city pumps along the way, women and servant girls chattered together as they drew the day's supply of water.

They passed delegates from the other colonies on their way to another session at Carpenter's Hall. The First Continental Congress had gathered in Philadelphia to decide on some course of action in America's struggle with England. The men wore serious expressions, as well they might. They were deciding the course of a nation.

And over the rooftops, David could see the masts of the huge sailing ships in the Delaware. This river path to the sea made Philadelphia a major seaport.

Down at the wharves, husky stevedores loaded and unloaded cargo while ships' captains bawled out orders. Winches creaked and workmen shouted.

Then the bells rang the hour of seven from Christ Church belfry, from St. Peter's, and from the high tower of the State House.

The city was a medley of movement and sound.

Above in the morning sky, a bright September sun promised another fair day. These early fall days were fine now, neither hot nor cold. And this was a special day for David, more wonderful than any other. He was going to the New York Colony to visit his aunt and uncle. They had invited him to spend two weeks with them, and he had

CHRIST CHURCH, PHILADELPHIA, IN 1776

persuaded his parents to let him go. He was on his way to the village of Brooklyn. This would be his first time away from home and, more than that, his first ride in a stagecoach. He was excited and just a bit frightened.

"Hurry along, David!" his mother commanded. "The stage departs promptly at eight! Let's hope we can get you aboard."

Three days each week a coach set out from the Barley Sheaf Tavern on Second Street bound for New York. It operated on a "first come, first served" basis. When available space was sold out, tardy passengers had to wait until the next scheduled journey. The trip took two days, an incredible speed in eighteenth-century America. Most stagecoach journeys were much longer. The trip from Boston to New York could take over one week and the trip between Philadelphia and Baltimore took five days!

The Swift-Sure Line traveled over the York Road, a crude highway linking Philadelphia and New York. This was the shortest and fastest overland route between the two cities. The Pennsylvania section was begun in 1711 and the New Jersey section was completed by 1764.

It was then that John Butler boldly announced that he was establishing an "Express" stagecoach service over the road, and that the trip would take just two days! To emphasize such remarkable speed, he named his coaches the "Flying Machines"!

"We're almost there," his mother said. As they turned a corner, David caught sight of the tavern sign. Made of heavy oak, it hung suspended from an iron bracket. On it was printed the picture of a golden sheaf of barley. Beyond

it, he could see the Sign of the Bunch of Grapes. Colonial inns and taverns, like their counterparts in England, had interesting and colorful names. His favorite inn sign in Philadelphia was the "Man Full of Trouble." It pictured an old man with a sad expression on his face—a man full of trouble!

Reaching their destination, the two walked inside and entered the common room. This was similar to a present day hotel lobby.

Many of the other passengers had already arrived. Horsehide chests, wooden boxes, and leather bags were scattered about the room. There was much confusion as the passengers talked together or made inquiries of the Swift-Sure agent. He was seated behind a small table, and on the wall behind him a poster announced:

> The Swift-Sure stage will leave
> the Barley Sheaf at eight in the
> morning bound for New York by
> way of Elizabethtown. It will arrive
> at Well's Ferry nine hours later.
> There will be stops for refresh-
> ments and changing of horses ev-
> ery ten miles.
>
> Our route over the York Road is
> through the finest, most pleasant,
> and best inhabited part of the country.
>
> Our Flying Machine is a coach
> brought from England equipt with
> springs to afford the utmost comfort.
>
> Fare, twenty shillings.
> Passengers going part of the
> way to pay in proportion.

To the PUBLIC.

THE FLYING MACHINE, kept by John Mercereau, at the New Blazing-Star-Ferry, near New-York, sets off from Powles Hook every Monday, Wednesday, and Friday Mornings, for Philadelphia, and performs the Journey in a Day and a Half, for the Summer Season, till the 1st of November; from that Time to go twice a Week till the first of May, when they again perform it three Times a Week. When the Stages go only twice a Week, they set off Mondays and Thursdays. The Waggons in Philadelphia set out from the Sign of the George, in Second-street, the same Morning. The Passengers are desired to cross the Ferry the Evening before, as the Stages must set off early the next Morning The Price for each Passenger is *Twenty Shillings*, Proc. and Goods as usual. Passengers going Part of the Way to pay in Proportion.

As the Proprietor has made such Improvements upon the Machines, one of which is in Imitation of a Coach, he hopes to merit the Favour of the Publick.

JOHN MERCEREAU.

1

"Have you space for one small boy?" David's mother asked the agent.

"I do, madame," he answered. "And you can rest certain that he will have a safe and pleasant journey."

She paid the agent the twenty shillings. Then, handing David a small pouch of coins, she instructed, "This will pay for your meals along the way. Always count your change and allow no one to cheat you!"

David nodded as he carefully placed the pouch in his coat pocket.

"And mind the coachman!" his mother continued.

"Yes, mother," David promised.

Like the captain of a ship, the coachman's word was law during the journey. He was treated with great respect. Driving a coach was considered so fine an art that, today, we use the word "coach" for a person who directs an athletic team or prepares someone for a difficult task.

As they stood there, a round-faced woman approached.

"Where is your boy going?" she inquired of David's mother.

"Bound for New York to visit relatives," Mrs. Wicks answered.

"I, too, am going to New York," the woman responded. "My sister and I are hairdressers and we hope to find work there. That young man is also traveling to New York," she continued, pointing out a lanky youth in rumpled clothing. "He is a schoolmaster who hopes to take a school on Long Island."

Mrs. Wicks smiled.

"And that man over there is a merchant and the one with him is a minister." She seemed to have made it her business to know everyone and their destinations.

"Then David will be traveling in good company," Mrs. Wicks remarked.

At that, an old man with shaggy grey hair entered the common room. He walked with a cane and carried a carpet bag.

Approaching the Swift-Sure agent, he shouted, "M' name is Elias Tweed. What's the fare to Quibbletown in the Jersey colony?"

"Fifteen shillings, sir," the agent told him.

"Fifteen shillings!" the old man exploded. "We need not fear the Doanes with bandits like you to rob us!"

The Doane Brothers were notorious outlaws who tormented the middle colonies. They frequently stopped stagecoaches to rob the passengers.

"Not only that," the agent explained. "You'll have to walk from the road into the village. The stage does not go through Quibbletown."

The old man snorted, as he reluctantly counted out the necessary shillings.

Then he sat down on a bench next to David and his mother to await the arrival of the coach.

Meanwhile, in the stables behind the inn, ostlers and stable boys were hitching the horses and preparing the coach for its journey. They adjusted the harnesses and polished the exterior of the coach with thick woolen pads. This was the famous Flying Machine and it had to look its best on the road.

The Journey Begins

The tall mahogany clock in the corner of the common room chimed the hour of eight. Precisely at the final stroke, a great rumble was heard in the street as the Swift-Sure coach rolled from the stable to the tavern door.

"Late as usual!" the old man complained as he glanced at a big gold watch extracted from his vest pocket.

"Late, Mr. Tweed?" the agent remarked, overhearing him. "The Swift-Sure is never late! We pride ourselves on keeping to schedule. It is your timepiece that must be out of tune."

Then, he stood up and, placing his hands to his mouth, called out, "The Swift-Sure Stage to New York departing at once! All passengers assemble!"

There was a sudden flurry of activity as the passengers gathered their belongings and hurried outside. David and his mother followed, with David clutching the leather handle of a round wooden box. It was his mother's hatbox, but it would serve as his traveling case.

Once outside, he beheld the breathtaking sight of the gleaming coach and the four speckled horses pulling it. Their harnesses jingled as they pawed nervously on the cobblestones. Their heads bobbed up and down in an incoherent rhythm.

The coach itself was a bright black conveyance resting on four great spoked wheels. It had four open windows, two on either side, with tall doors between. Each window had a leather curtain that was rolled up and secured at top. These could be lowered in bad weather. Inside, there were padded leather seats that would take six to eight passengers, depending on their size. One seat faced forward and the other faced backward. On the coach doors, in fancy gold lettering, was printed—The Flying Machine—Philadelphia to New York.

To young David, the coach looked as wonderful and as exciting as a rocket to the moon might look to us.

Busy ostlers and stable boys lifted and strapped the luggage to the flat roof of the coach where a low brass railing prevented it from sliding off.

And, on a high seat up front, called the box, sat the coachman. He was a huge man with a genial face and a round stomach. He wore dark breeches and coat, a bright red vest, and a tall hat with a tiny feather stuck in the band.

"Ladies and Gentlemen, I am John Watson, your coach-man!" he bellowed in a deep voice. Then he spit down onto the cobblestones. "Please follow all my instructions during the journey!" He tugged the reins gently and snapped his leather whip in the air. The horses grew more nervous, awaiting the command to pull away.

Then, looking down at David, he called out, "Here, there, lad! Climb up next to me. You can blow the coach horn for me." Resting at his side was a long brass horn, used to signal the stage's approach. David could hardly believe his ears. What a privilege it was to be asked to sit with the coachman.

"Take care, David," his mother said as she kissed him good-bye. Then she helped him up onto the box.

Meanwhile the other passengers boarded, helped up the small folding steps by the Swift-Sure agent. One of the lad-ies handed him a coin.

"Thank ye, madame!"

"Forgive me for saying it, sir," the agent said addressing the schoolmaster, "but as you are the thinnest, you should sit in the middle."

"I need air!" old Tweed growled as he plopped himself next to a window.

The two ladies busied themselves tucking a blanket around their legs while the minister mumbled a silent prayer for a safe journey.

When everyone was settled, the agent folded the steps and closed the door. He made a final check of the horses and harness. Satisfied that all was right, he called out, "All ready, inside and out!"

"Let 'em go then!" the coachman roared. Cracking his whip, the coach clattered away. They were off! John Watson took the horn and put it to his lips. Ta-ta! Ta-ta!

The notes of the horn, the jingle of harness, and the clatter of the wheels warned everyone that the Swift-Sure was on its way. David glanced back and saw his mother waving her handkerchief. But he was afraid to return her farewell. The bouncing and swaying of the coach made him hold on for dear life. He huddled next to the coachman.

Down the streets of old Philadelphia they went, past Christ Church, Walnut Street, then High Street. The neat brick houses and the quaint shops of the city whizzed by. Pigs squealed as they ran from the path of the coach and,

here and there, neighborhood dogs raced alongside bark-
ing at the horses. Children playing in the streets shouted
and waved. Again the coachman blew his horn. Ta-ta! Ta-
ta!

After passing Vine Street, the coach turned onto the
York Road. Suddenly the city was gone. Now, in place
of busy streets they traveled through open countryside.
The cobblestones had turned to dirt and clouds of dust rose
behind them.

"Here, lad," the coachman said handing David the horn.
"See if you can give 'er a toot!"

David took the horn and put it to his lips. A weak squeal
ensued.

"Purse your lips, take a deep breath, and try again,"
John Watson instructed.

David filled his lungs and blew into the horn. This
second try was better than the first.

"Again!" John Watson ordered.

At the third try, much to his delight, a clear ta-ta came
out.

"Good lad!" complimented the coachman. "Now,
whenever I nudge you with my elbow, blow out!"

"Yes sir!" David answered with a smile. He was begin-
ning to relax and enjoy the ride.

Inside the coach, the other passengers were being
bounced and jolted unmercifully. Old Mr. Tweed shouted
out the window, "Slow down, ya fool! My bones are rat-
tling in my skin!" But the coachman ignored him. The
comfort of their passengers was of little concern to most

drivers. To hold to their schedules was the main consideration and John Watson was no exception. He was renowned for his punctuality.

The stage hit a rut in the road and David bounced high in his seat.

"That was a bad one," the coachman admitted.

The roads of colonial America were little more than wide dirt paths. All the roads were dusty in dry weather and muddy in wet. In winter snows, they were impassable. Traveling over the York Road today, as it now exists as a modern highway, motorists might find it difficult to imagine the discomfort of road travel in 1774.

The removal of tree stumps and boulders during the road's construction left holes to be filled with dirt. These became mud holes during the rainy season. Some holes were so bad that split tree trunks had to be laid over them. Certain very poor sections of the road had over a quarter of a mile of these split log coverings. These were appropriately called, "corduroy roads."

One tall tale had it that a certain rut in the York Road was so deep that four coaches, two wagons, and a herd of sheep fell into it and disappeared. Of course, this was not true. The story merely exaggerated the poor condition of the road.

Suddenly David felt a sharp nudge at his side. He quickly picked up the stage horn and blew. Ta-ta! Ta-ta! It was a warning to a farmer up ahead who was walking his cattle along the road. The frightened animals scurried to the sides as the coach roared by.

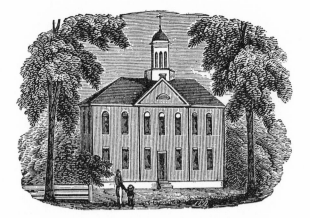

Not satisfied with their progress, John Watson cracked his whip. "Git up there, Joey! Do your share of the pulling, Ben!" The horses picked up speed.

They rushed by a country church. Its slender white steeple rose from behind the trees. They sped past fieldstone houses and barns. The fall morning was growing more golden as the sun climbed into the sky. And the leaves had begun to turn, forming a colorful arch along the road.

The rush of the cool air against his face, the jogging of the coach, the unfamiliar countryside, and the motion of the galloping horses created an excitement that David had never before experienced. And his journey had just begun!

A Change of Horses

As the Swift-Sure stagecoach sped along the York Road, John Watson called out his orders. As they rounded one bend he shouted, "Lean to the left!" At another, "Lean to the right!"

Passengers were expected to shift their weight from side to side in order to keep the stage balanced. Otherwise, the coach might topple over. This is where we got the expression, "to throw your weight around." It is used today to describe the actions of a person who uses the power of his position. In coaching days, throwing your weight around was an important function, especially for the heavier passengers.

About ten o'clock in the morning, two hours and twelve miles out of Philadelphia, the coach neared the tiny village of Abington. A nudge from John Watson and a ta-ta on the horn from David announced their arrival at the village inn. Here, horses would be changed and passengers refreshed.

These coaching stops were generally called "taverns" in New York and New Jersey and called "inns" in Pennsylvania. In the South they were known as "ordinaries."

The typical inn in 1774 consisted of a large common

room with a fireplace. Here the innkeeper had his desk.
The room also served as a drinking place. In one corner
there was a simple bar where drinks were dispensed. On
the ground floor, were also a small dining room and a
kitchen. On the second floor, there were several sleeping
rooms, depending on the size of the building. And behind
the inn, there was a large stable for the horses.

Warned by the sound of the horn, the innkeeper and his
staff prepared for the approaching stagecoach. The stable
hands ran out to meet it.

As the coach came to a halt before the inn, the horses
were visibly exhausted. Their coats were white with lather
and their sides heaved in and out. They were quickly unhitched and led away.

"Good morning, Captain," called the innkeeper.

A fresh four-horse team was already waiting.

Two leaders and two wheelers made up the usual coach
team and they were changed about every ten miles. Ten
miles of fast running and heavy pulling was about all a
healthy horse could endure. Unfortunately, many coach

horses were often mistreated. Whipped into going faster and faster and forced to pull up steep hills, many horses became sick or lame. Often a horse was driven so hard during a journey that he died. Another expression, "to die in harness" comes from these times.

Dropping his reins, John Watson climbed down from the box, leaving the coach to the ostler's care. David followed. The other passengers climbed out of the coach, already weary from the first part of their journey. Old Mr. Tweed ran to the backyard privy, while the others went inside for refreshments.

"Come on, lad!" John Watson said to David, throwing his arm around his shoulder. "We'll go in and have something to drink to wash the dust of the road from our throats." They walked together into the common room, the coachman swaggering like a lord.

"You there!" he called to a serving girl. "Two pints of cider!"

By now, the other passengers knew each other by name. The minister was Mr. Tate; the merchant, Mr. Kirk; the schoolmaster, Mr. Jeffers; and the two ladies, Miss Martha and Miss Ruth. As they sat talking together, old Tweed appeared banging his cane on the floor.

"A mug of tea!" he shouted. "And some buttered bread!"

"Drink it down fast, Mr. Tweed," John Watson warned. "This is a short stop. We leave as soon as the horses are hitched."

"I hope it's not English tea!" Miss Martha remarked.

DESTRUCTION OF THE TEA AT BOSTON

"Certainly not, madame," Mr. Kirk laughed. "Most of that has been dumped into Philadelphia and Boston harbors!"

"Let's hope that the Congress can solve our problems over these terrible taxes," Miss Ruth sighed.

"They will drag us into war over it," Mr. Tweed snorted. "You can't defy the King and not ask for bloodshed, that's what I say!"

"Enough political talk!" John Watson ordered. "We are almost ready to go. Drink up!" He drained his mug of cider. David watched as the serving girls and the innkeeper rushed about the room serving the customers.

The smooth working of the stage system depended greatly on the efficiency of the inns. In a system which demanded a quick change of horses, there was no room for slow service. An innkeeper who tolerated slowness would not last long. His staff, like the coach horses, had to be whipped into efficiency.

The inns had no set hours. They were open around the clock. Sometimes the stops by travelers were brief. At other times, passengers had to be served a hot meal or bedded down for the night.

But the inn was not only a stage stop. It also served as a meeting place for the surrounding community. People gathered together to talk and enjoy themselves. Often, dances and social affairs were held at the inns. And inns and taverns played an important role in politics. As the center of community social life, it was only natural that the inns served as a meeting place for political activity. Long before the start of the Revolution, the Sons of Liberty held their meetings at inns throughout the colonies. Eventually, Thomas Jefferson would write the Declaration of Independence in the Indian Queen Tavern in Philadelphia.

Outside, the coach was checked by the stable hands. The wheels were examined to be certain they were secure on the axles. The harnesses were checked and the fresh horses were given a final brushing.

"All ready, Captain!" a hand called in to John Watson.

Hearing this, the passengers gulped down their drinks. Mr. Tweed dipped the last crust of his buttered bread into his tea and popped it into his mouth.

David reached into his pocket and pulled out the leather pouch of coins that his mother had given him.

"How much do I owe you for the cider, sir?" he asked the innkeeper.

"Save your coins, lad," John Watson interrupted. "The cider can be charged to my account!" He winked at the innkeeper who smiled back. A coachman was rarely charged for anything at the stops. It was good business to take care of the coachman!

"Thank you, sir!" David answered as he carefully returned the pouch to his pocket.

Then all walked outside to board the coach. A fresh team of horses was hitched to the coach. These new animals were chestnuts and their coats glistened in the morning sunlight.

John Watson climbed back onto the box and extended a hand to David. Mr. Kirk and Mr. Tate helped the ladies aboard and Mr. Jeffers gave his arm to Tweed. All settled, the coach door was shut and secured.

John Watson took the reins and tested their tautness. Satisfied, he nodded to the hands that he was ready to go.

"Give 'er a blow, lad!" he said.

David put the horn to his lips and blew into it.

Ta-ta! Ta-ta-ta!

The coach was off!

At first, John Watson kept his horses at a steady trot. Then, he snapped his whip to bring them to a gallop. The four sets of reins, one for each horse, were laced between his fingers. He had perfect control of each animal, and he manipulated the reins with ease and comfort. Now and then he would crack the whip above the head of a horse that wasn't pulling well. He sent it out snaking and hissing in the air. A good coachman never lashed his horses. He

used the whip as a symbol of his authority. The worst he gave them was a slight sting from the tip to urge them to their best efforts.

They passed through village after village. Quaker ladies in grey dresses waved, dogs barked, children shouted, and farmers stopped work in the fields to watch them pass by.

The countryside they passed through was lush. Thick stands of trees covered the hillsides and clear streams and brooks crisscrossed the land. William Penn had written, "This place is good, the air is sweet and clear, the water plentiful and the woods thick." As they rolled along through Penn's Province, David could only agree. He looked up into the blue sky and saw that the sun was approaching its peak. It was almost noon.

Too Much Gingerbread

Ten miles of hard driving since their last stop brought the Swift-Sure coach to the village of Crossroads. Here, the Easton-Bristol Road crossed the York Road. This was the noonday stop for coach and passengers.

A short distance from the village, John Watson informed David that he would blow the horn for this stop.

"Have to let old Will at the Heart know that I expect my stew to be ready!"

He put the horn to his lips and his blast made David's amateur notes sound pitiful.

Ta-da-da-da—Ta Ta! Ta-da-da-da—Ta Ta!

The curiosity of the other passengers was aroused. They stuck their heads out of the windows to see what was happening.

John Watson blew again.

Ta-da-da-da—Ta Ta! Ta-da-da-da—Ta Ta!

They rushed up to the Sign of the Heart and came to a screeching halt. The tavern sign with its picture of a red heart swayed in the wake of the coach.

The innkeeper, a jolly man with a round, ruddy face, stood in the doorway.

"You make enough noise to wake the dead, John Watson," he called out.

"Just enough to get you moving, William Hart! I've got a load of hungry passengers and four tired horses for you!"

"Come inside, all of you!" the innkeeper answered. "My kitchen is bursting with good food!" And indeed it was!

Once inside, the passengers were welcomed by a variety of sweet smells and savory odors. David recognized the familiar scents of hot gingerbread and steaming apples. It made him a bit homesick for his mother's kitchen back in Philadelphia.

On the wall was a wooden sign with a listing of the tavern's offerings. David read it carefully.

> Here is Drink for the Thirsty, Food for the Hungry, Lodging for the Weary, and Good Keeping for Horses.

Jug of Cider	4 pence
Jug of Common Beer or Ale	5 pence
Pint of West Indies Rum	11 pence
Bread and Butter	2 pence
Sweet Breads and Butter	4 pence
Pot luck per meal	1 shilling 8 pence
Slices of Venison or Ham	6 pence
Stewed Fruits or Vegetables	3 pence
Common Lodging	1 shilling 5 pence
Horses or Other Animals	3 pence

"Have a bowl of the pot luck stew, lad," John Watson advised. "It's the best in the province!"

The ride and the fresh air had made David quite hungry, so he ordered the stew and a jug of cider.

All the passengers sat at a common table. Mr. Jeffers, the schoolmaster, sat on David's right and Mr. Kirk, the merchant, sat on his left. Across from him sat Miss Martha, Miss Ruth, and Mr. Tate. Tweed sat at one end of the table and John Watson at the other. They were a family of travelers.

"So you are going to visit your relatives, young man?" Miss Ruth inquired.

"Yes, ma'am," David answered politely. "My uncle and aunt live in New York and they invited me to visit them. I am happy that mama and papa agreed to let me go."

There was more conversation. Talk about politics, city life, and the sights along the way. The arrival of the stagecoach at any stop was an eventful occurrence since the coaches brought news and travelers from the outside world. John Watson had even brought along a copy of the

Pennsylvania Gazette for the innkeeper. It was the first Philadelphia newspaper the man had seen in over a week and he was anxious to read about the Continental Congress. In the tiny hamlet of Crossroads, the events taking place in Philadelphia made interesting reading and generated much discussion.

Conversation ceased when the steaming bowls of stew were brought to the table along with breads and fruits.

"This is an excellent stew," Miss Martha announced sampling a mouthful. "But it needs a bit more spice."

"Spice is bad for your stomach, madame," Mr. Tate responded.

"Beg to disagree with you, but it is my opinion that this stew needs spice!" Miss Martha insisted.

To David, the stew was just right. It tasted delicious. And with it, he ate four slices of gingerbread and three honey cakes.

"Take it easy, lad!" John Watson advised. "The bounces and bumps of the York Road are hard on a full stomach. And the worst stretch is still before us."

David did not listen. The food was too good and he was too hungry. He ate another slice of buttered gingerbread.

"The boy will be sick!" Miss Martha warned.

But David had paid for his meal and was getting his money's worth.

The stop at the Sign of the Heart lasted one hour. It was a welcome break in the journey as there were still nine hours to travel this first day.

The time passed quickly and soon the stage was ready to depart.

"See you on my return trip," John Watson called to the innkeeper. "I may even bring you a newspaper from New York!"

With that, they departed and the fresh horses seemed to have more energy than any team so far. They raced down the road raising heavy clouds of dust behind them. The coach bounced and swayed. David felt a bit uneasy, and he wished that he had not eaten that last slice of gingerbread!

A short distance out of Crossroads, they passed women carrying baskets on their heads and men wheeling barrows. They had been to market in one of the villages and were returning home. They also passed several lime wagons and a farmer driving a herd of goats.

Then, in the distance, David saw what appeared to be another stagecoach.

"Ha-ha!" John Watson exclaimed. "There's Amos Turner's coach up ahead!"

Amos Turner operated a coach between Crooked Billet

and Well's Ferry. As this covered part of the route of the Swift-Sure, he was considered a competitor.

"We'll show him why we're called the Flying Machines!" John Watson shouted as he snapped his whip over the horses. The animals seemed to sense the urgency of the moment. They increased their speed and the coach whizzed along the road. Within minutes, it was almost on top of the other coach.

"Move over and let me pass!" John Watson called to the other coachman.

"Stay where you are or fly over me with your machine!" Amos Turner laughed.

David saw John Watson's face grow red with anger. He snapped his whip again and edged the coach alongside the other. There was not sufficient room for the two coaches and each one had to edge close to the side of the narrow road.

"Stop this madness!" Tweed shouted from inside. "You'll kill us all!"

The two coaches raced along, side by side. Occasionally they bumped into each other, and David was afraid they would topple over. They were unmercifully banged and bounced. The women began to scream. But John Watson was determined to win the race. Once again he snapped his whip and the frothing horses surged ahead.

Seeing that it was useless to continue this match, Amos Turner called out, "I give up! Go ahead!" He reined his team. With that, the Flying Machine raced by leaving its competition far behind.

But the excitement and action of the race had been too much for David. He tugged at John Watson's coat. "I think I'm going to be sick," he said. They slowed to a stop and David rushed into the bushes.

"I knew the boy would be sick!" Miss Martha commented.

"Too much hot gingerbread," Mr. Kirk added.

"Rather too much tomfoolery!" Mr. Tweed complained. "It's small wonder we are not all sick, or dead! If there is much more of this, I shall walk the rest of the way!"

John Watson threw back his head and laughed. He had enjoyed the race and the opportunity to demonstrate his coaching skill.

Crossing the Delaware

Shortly past three in the afternoon, the Swift-Sure stage reached Bogart's Tavern at Buckingham. This too was a crossroads village. At Buckingham, the Durham Road crossed the York Road. Again, this was a short stop for a change of horses. This is what "stagecoach" meant—a journey by coach done in stages.

From Buckingham, the coach headed toward Well's Ferry and the Delaware. By now, David was feeling much better and had resolved never to overeat again. At Bogart's he had had a mug of milk and rum, a remedy suggested by Miss Ruth.

The coach bounced along the dirt road to the sound of those familiar instructions—Lean to the right! Lean to the left! It rolled through the hamlet of Lahaska where a small band of Leni-Lenape Indians lived. The following year, they would leave Pennsylvania and journey westward. Then, the coach passed the Great Spring, called Aquetong by the Indians. The size of a lake, this spring is the largest on the East Coast. It produces over a million gallons of water each day. David saw some Indian squaws on the far bank washing clothing.

Three miles beyond the Great Spring, the York Road

turned, went through a small valley and then descended sharply toward Well's Ferry and the river. Here, the mighty Delaware formed a natural barrier between Pennsylvania and New Jersey.

The Delaware flows from north to south between Pennsylvania and New Jersey. Before it reaches the sea, it curves to pass the city of Philadelphia. In days past, the journey to Well's Ferry might have been taken by boat up the Delaware. But, by 1774, overland travel was quicker and more convenient. So, one left the Delaware at Philadelphia only to meet it again upstream at Well's Ferry.

On the New Jersey side of the river, the ferry was called Coryell's Ferry. John Wells operated the ferry service from Pennsylvania to New Jersey and George Coryell was licensed to run it in the opposite direction.

David signaled the coach's arrival on the horn and, shortly thereafter, John Watson halted the Flying Machine before the Logan Inn. This inn, also owned by John Wells, was named in honor of William Penn's secretary, James Logan.

"You can stretch your legs here for awhile," John Watson told the passengers, "while I make arrangements for our crossing at the toll house."

"Come on, lad," he said to David, "you can come with me."

The two walked toward the riverfront and entered a small stone building.

"When can you take us across?" John Watson inquired of a young man seated at a high desk.

"Soon as you're ready," he answered lazily.

"How's the river today?"

"Running a bit fast," the young man replied. "May take a trifle longer."

At the inn, stable hands unhitched the team and pushed the empty coach to the river bank. Fresh horses would be waiting on the other side.

"Run back to the inn, lad, and tell our passengers to get down here," John Watson instructed. "We leave as soon as that coach is secured on the flatboat."

David hurried back to the inn with the coachman's message.

The ferryboats were large flatboats, much like barges. They were equipped with hinged flaps at either end which, when lowered to the riverbank, allowed the coach to be rolled aboard. Once on the ferry, leather straps placed through the wheels held the coach firm. This prevented it from moving during the crossing.

In 1774, there were no large bridges and most rivers had to be crossed by boat. For a set fee, a ferry would transport anything from a stagecoach to a herd of animals.

"Come on!" John Watson called out, as David and the other passengers hurried toward the ferry. When they were all aboard, the order was given.

"Cast off!"

Using a long pole, the ferryman pushed the boat from the riverbank. Then, with the help of another man using a similar pole, the boat was pushed and steered across the Delaware. It was hard work as they had to fight the water's current yet keep their proper direction. Being a ferryman was a highly skilled occupation. The two men dug their poles into the river's bed and pushed the boat along. Their muscles strained.

The river seemed much bigger out in the middle. The shorelines were heavily wooded and downstream the Delaware seemed to melt into a rise of low hills. Overhead, hawks circled in the sky.

"This is a lovely river," Mr. Jeffers remarked. "I was here once before many years ago. The shad were running at the time, and I watched fishermen actually scoop them out of the river in bushel baskets!"

"Yes, and I am told that there is plentiful deer and bear on both shores," Mr. Kirk added.

Suddenly, a shout interrupted their conversation.

"Throw the rope!"

It came from a man on shore. They had less than twenty feet to go. Within minutes, they were safely moored on the New Jersey shore.

"First time I ever set foot in another colony!" David exclaimed as he stepped from the boat.

"Best province in all the colonies, in my opinion!" said Mr. Tweed.

Looking back across the river, Philadelphia and home seemed far, far away. Actually, they had traveled only thirty-three miles!

On to Larrison's

On the New Jersey side of the river the land seemed much flatter and the road much smoother.

Actually, the Jersey section of the York Road had utilized large stretches of roads already existing between villages and these were kept in good condition. Also, the farmers living along the York Road could work off part of their land taxes by keeping the road in repair. Because of this, the York Road in New Jersey was better graded and had fewer ruts.

By the time the Swift-Sure coach reached Mount Airy, the sun was low on the horizon. By the time it passed through the village of Ringoes, the windows of the village houses had turned to gold in the reflection of the setting sun. Beyond Ringoes was the next stage stop—Pleasant Corners.

One of the largest and most popular taverns on the York Road was situated in Pleasant Corners. The entire lower floor of Larrison's Tavern could be converted into a ballroom by folding back movable partitions. There were frequent dances and parties there, making Larrison's an interesting stop. Often the stagecoach passengers were invited to join in the fun.

"Give it a loud toot, lad!" John Watson said. "Maybe there is a party going on at Larrison's and we want them to know we're coming!"

David attempted to imitate John Watson.

Ta-da-da! Ta-da-da!

The sound wasn't the same, but it was better than usual!

Sure enough, when they got to Larrison's, a dance was in progress. All the rooms of the tavern glowed brightly in the evening twilight and the strains of music broke the stillness of the countryside. As the main meal in colonial times was taken at midday, it was not unusual for an evening's entertainment to be underway by late afternoon.

"We'll stop here a bit longer than usual," John Watson declared. "I'll make up the time down the road."

David was delighted with his decision as he had never been to a dance before.

Inside, the big room was crowded with people. On the far side, on a low wooden platform, there were three musicians with fiddles. They were playing melodic waltzes and highland reels. Gaily dressed ladies fluttered their fans as they glided across the floor with their partners. And many of the men, made too warm by rum and waltzing, wiped their brows with linen kerchiefs.

A young gentleman asked Miss Ruth to dance, and Mr. Jeffers discovered a pretty girl with long blonde curls.

At a table in another part of the room, John Watson entertained a group of men with some wild coaching stories while old Tweed argued politics with the innkeeper. It was a jolly time, and David was fascinated with the music and the dancing.

Suddenly, Miss Martha approached and asked him to dance with her.

"Don't know how, ma'am!" David replied.

"There's nothing to it, boy," she said. "Just take my hands and follow me!"

She twirled him around and round to the notes of a waltz until he was almost dizzy. Wouldn't his mother be surprised, he thought, if she could see him now!

While they were still dancing, they heard the coachman's voice rise above the music.

"All Swift-Sure passengers! Board the coach!"

Their stay at Larrison's was over, and the last stage of their day's journey was before them. Outside a bright autumn moon illuminated the sky. John Watson stood by the coach swinging a lantern while a stable hand gave a final check to the harnesses.

With many waves and shouts of good-bye from the remaining guests, the Swift-Sure pulled away from Larrison's Tavern and headed down the moonlit road.

Without any instruction from the coachman, David picked up the coach horn and blew a farewell note.

Ta-ta! Ta-ta!

John Watson smiled as he cracked his whip over the team. They had time to make up if they wanted to reach Centerville by ten.

Overnight at Centerville

The first day of the journey was almost over. In a few short hours it would be midnight and the start of a new day. A bright moon in a star-speckled sky promised another fine morning.

Except for the noise of the coach and the occasional baying of a wolf in the distance, the night was still. Here and there, a farmhouse window flickered with candlelight, but most of the countryside was asleep.

The night air, as it brushed his face, was chilly and pungent with the damp odors of forest and farm.

David wished that he were back in Philadelphia, snug in his bed. By this time he would have been long asleep. But, instead, he was riding along a highway in the wilds of New Jersey. His home and his parents seemed so far away. The passing of time had exaggerated the separation.

Another wolf howled in the forest and David moved closer to John Watson.

Before long, the coach rounded a bend in the road and David saw lights in the distance. It was the welcoming blaze of candles and lanterns. With bright moonlight and fast driving, John Watson had managed to reach Centerville on schedule.

The Stage House at Centerville was the overnight stop for the Swift-Sure stagecoaches.

Centerville, so named because it was the center point in the journey, was a tiny village. It had a few houses, a blacksmith shop, and a general store. The largest building in the village was the Stage House, owned and operated by the Swift-Sure Line. The overnight stay here was included in the fare.

By now, David and the other passengers were tired and hungry. It had been an exhausting trip. They had been on the road for fourteen hours.

David yawned as he climbed down from the box and entered the inn. His legs ached and his bottom was sore from bumping on the hard seat. He was tired and sore and ready for bed!

The innkeeper and his wife had prepared a supper for the expected travelers. A long cloth-covered table in the common room was an inviting sight, with its platters

of beef and ham, wheels of cheeses, and baskets of fruit. And a roaring log fire sent out a cheery glow from the huge fireplace. All in all, it was quite cozy indeed. The Stage House was renowned for its hospitality.

When supper was over, the innkeeper assigned rooms and beds to his guests. The two ladies were given separate quarters but the men had to share a common bedroom. More than this, they had to share beds.

This was not uncommon in 1774. With limited space, the luxury of a single bed or a private room was simply not available. Guests had to sleep two or three to a bed in rooms crowded with eight or ten beds.

No one undressed but signs on the walls asked that men "remove their boots before retiring."

It is said that Thomas Jefferson always traveled with a linen sleeping bag to slip into when he shared a bed with a stranger. To refuse to share a bed was considered rude and uncivilized.

David's name was the last to be mentioned. He heard the innkeeper say, "You and the old man can share a bed." Old Tweed was to be his bed partner!

They went upstairs by candlelight and entered a large dormitory room. Here they found a row of wooden beds. The beds were small but they had thick feather mattresses and feather pillows. Each bed had a single woolen blanket.

Mr. Tweed removed his coat and hung it on a peg in the wall. Then he pulled off his boots and climbed under the blanket.

"Well, get in, boy!" he said to David. David, now ready

for bed himself, lay down next to him. He tugged on the blanket.

"Stop that!" Tweed grumbled. "A boy your size doesn't need much cover!" He jerked the blanket leaving David uncovered.

"Excuse me, sir," David whispered. "But I have nothing now."

"Don't be sassy to your elders!" Tweed answered. "Go to sleep! And don't try to steal the blanket from me during the night!"

Before too long, Mr. Tweed was snoring loudly. So was John Watson who was sharing the next bed with Mr. Kirk. Tweed thrashed about, once almost pushing David to the floor.

Unable to sleep, David rested quietly in the darkness. The room grew cold and he reached over to reclaim a portion of blanket. He pulled on it gently so as not to awaken the old man. But it was no use! Tweed had tucked the cover under his chin and grasped it with tightly clenched fists. Even in sleep he refused to share it.

Once again, David's thoughts returned home to Philadelphia. Suddenly, in the loneliness of the night, he grew terribly homesick. The only cure was to close his eyes and force sleep. It worked, and in a little while he was dreaming of his day on the York Road.

It was still dark when the innkeeper called to awaken them. Outside, David could hear the creak of the coach as the horses were being hitched and the shouts of the stable hands.

He got out of bed and splashed some cold water on his face from a bowl and pitcher. Then he dried off with a small towel. Meanwhile, the men shaved by candlelight, sharing a single looking glass, while Tweed complained to everyone that he had not slept a wink all night.

Downstairs, the innkeeper had prepared a hearty breakfast of hot biscuits, johnnycakes, and sausages.

By eight o'clock, the sun blazed out of the east and poured through the windows of the tavern.

"Another fine day!" the innkeeper remarked.

And in the stable yard, the Flying Machine, now hitched to a team of anxiously prancing horses, glistened in the morning brilliance. The stable hands had polished it and rubbed away the grime and dust of the road. John Watson walked around the coach inspecting it in an aristocratic manner. Finally, he proclaimed it ready for the highway.

The passengers climbed aboard. Fortified with a night's sleep and a good breakfast, they made ready to embark on the second and final day of their journey on the York Road.

As the coach pulled away from Centerville, David blew the coach horn to signal their departure. Ta-ta! Ta-ta!

"Good-bye, Mr. Tweed"

From Centerville, the York Road went through the rolling countryside of the Raritan Valley. It passed lush farms and rich meadowland.

This part of New Jersey was inhabited by Dutch settlers who spoke their native language and wore their native clothing.

Near Somerville, the Flying Machine came upon two wagons drawn by teams of six draft horses. A Dutch family was moving to another farm and the wagons were piled high with all their belongings. There were gaily-painted Dutch cupboards, wooden chests, and chairs. And the family members were dressed in quaint costumes. The man wore a felt hat and baggy trousers. The woman and two young girls wore peaked lace caps. All of them wore wooden shoes. David had never seen this before. There were many Germans and Swedes in Philadelphia but very few immigrants from the Netherlands. The Dutch settled mainly in New Jersey and New York.

John Watson slowed the coach to ask if he might pass.

"*Neemt U my niet Kwalyk?*" he called.

"*Ja!*" the man answered as he pulled over to the side and waved him on.

"*Dank U!*" John Watson shouted.

"You speak their language!" David exclaimed, amazed at the coachman's knowledge.

"Remember, lad, that the colony of New York used to be called New Netherlands. I travel among these people all the time and I have learned some of their language. The Dutch have been here for over one hundred years!"

On down the road they sped until they reached the tiny village of Bound Brook. At Harris's Tavern they stopped for another change of horses. While there, David overheard the strange mixture of Dutch and English as people in the village met and talked together.

And John Watson pointed out an old house in the village that had been built on an Indian burying ground. He said that the house was haunted by the spirits of the redmen and that one of the children in the house had been carried away by an Indian ghost! It was a frightening story and David was relieved when the coach pulled out of Bound Brook.

Several miles from Bound Brook, John Watson halted the coach.

"Whoa, there, boys!" he called out as he pulled in the reins.

It was a lonely and deserted spot surrounded by tall trees and bushes. A narrow path led off one side of the road into the woods.

"Here you are, Mr. Tweed!" he called out. "That path over yonder leads to Quibbletown."

The door opened and Tweed climbed out of the coach.

"Had I suspected that my sister lived in the wilderness, I would not have bothered to visit her!" he grumbled.

Meanwhile, John Watson had climbed to the roof of the coach. He threw down Mr. Tweed's traveling bag.

"There you are, Mr. Tweed!" he said. "And be on the lookout for bears. The woods are full of them!"

Mr. Tweed, looking very annoyed and a little frightened, gathered himself together and started down the path. As he walked along, he beat away the overhanging branches with his cane.

"I think the bears should be warned about Mr. Tweed!" Miss Ruth said, laughing.

"He'll get there safely," John Watson assured everyone. "There are farmhouses along the way, and the village is not far."

"Good-bye, Mr. Tweed!" David called.

"Good-bye!" the others echoed as they waved.

The old man glanced over his shoulder and moved his hand in a reluctant farewell. On he went down the path until he disappeared from sight.

"One passenger safely delivered, but he leaves us with an empty seat!" John Watson remarked as he snapped the reins. With that, the Flying Machine continued on its journey.

The Swift-Sure Line was a through coach and preferred passengers who took the complete journey. Those traveling only part of the way, like Mr. Tweed, were not given priority when tickets were issued.

Politics

Before long, they reached the tavern at Scotch Plains. This was the scheduled noonday stop for dinner.

In 1684, some Scotch immigrants were looking for a place to settle and found a location in New Jersey to their liking. They made it their home. Later on, it was given the name Scotch Plains.

The tavern at Scotch Plains was small but comfortable. The innkeeper, a descendant of the original Scots, was a gracious host and had prepared a large dinner for the travelers. There were platters of ham and turkey and bowls of steaming vegetables. His wife had even made several pumpkin pies.

Following dinner, everyone sat around the table drinking mugs of spiced cider and talking together. Soon, the conversation turned to politics.

In 1774, two years before the signing of the Declaration of Independence, the political situation in the colonies was a vital issue. The disagreement with Great Britain and the burden of heavy taxation were topics of great interest to every citizen. And sentiments were divided. Not everyone considered independence a proper course. There were many people who were loyal to the English monarch.

The innkeeper, overhearing the discussion, joined the

group and supplied some interesting news.

"There was a man who stopped here yesterday," he told them, "who was on his way back from Philadelphia. Perhaps you passed him along the way. He was riding a black horse."

JohnWatson shook his head. He did not recall seeing him.

"He is an aide to Mr. William Livingston of Elizabethtown, one of Jersey's delegates to the Continental Congress. He told of hearing the Virginia delegate, a fellow named Patrick Henry, say, 'The distinctions between Virginians, Pennsylvanians, New Yorkers, New Englanders are no more. Boundaries are dissolved. I am not a Virginian, but an American!' "

"Well that may be fine for Mr. Henry," Mr. Kirk remarked, "but I am a Pennsylvanian and quite happy to stay that way!"

"The Congress is talking of us as one country instead of thirteen colonies!" the innkeeper added.

"One country, indeed!" sniffed Mr. Tate. "If they continue with this kind of talk, they'll have us all in trouble for sure!"

"It's not trouble to demand your rights!" argued Miss Martha.

The discussion continued with taxes, tariffs, and the English King loudly debated.

"What are the political sentiments here?" John Watson asked the innkeeper.

"We have many loyalists," he answered, "especially around Morristown. Most of the older folk want peace.

It's the young people who talk revolution and separation."

"Aye!" John Watson agreed as he shook his finger at David who sat across from him. "It's you young folk who make trouble!"

David blinked. "But I didn't do anything, sir," he protested. "I don't even know what the Congress is all about. I don't understand political matters."

"Shame on you!" scolded Miss Martha. "You should pay more attention and learn about your country!"

"That's right!" John Watson added. "You young people pay no heed to important matters!"

David lowered his eyes and decided that, at times, both adults and politics could be very confusing.

He was pleased when it came time to leave. The jingle of the horses' harness and the rattle of the Flying Machine were preferable to talk of the Continental Congress!

The day was cool and David pulled his coat closer to his body. The road now wound its way around the shoulders of low hills through thick woods of cedar and scrub pine. The Flying Machine thundered along the narrow, twisting road. David sensed that John Watson was concerned about being on schedule. The political talk at the inn had taken up too much time. Shouting and cracking his whip, the four high-spirited bays now pulling the coach galloped faster and faster. The coach rocked and lurched behind them and the passengers bumped up and down in their seats.

Benjamin Franklin once said that lost time is hard to find; but, John Watson was certainly trying!

By Ferry to New York

By midafternoon, the Swift-Sure coach reached Elizabeth-town. It roared past small cottages and stately homes until it reached the Indian Queen Tavern. Here, Mr. Kirk and Mr. Tate concluded their journey on the Flying Machine. They planned to transfer to another coach that would take them to Newark and the Powles Hook (Jersey City) Ferry. From Powles Hook, it was a short trip across the Hudson to New York. The others planned to take the Elizabethtown Ferry, two miles down the road, all the way to New York.

David said good-bye to his traveling companions and helped with their luggage.

"We would rather go by way of Powles Hook," Mr. Kirk explained. "A lengthy water voyage is not to our liking and Powles Hook is more convenient to our destination."

The two men entered the Indian Queen to await the arrival of the second coach. This coach was operated by a private line serving points in northern New Jersey.

Meanwhile, the Flying Machine bolted away to complete its journey.

"Give her a last toot, lad!" John Watson ordered as they neared the wharf.

David placed the coach horn to his lips to play the final notes.

Ta-da-da! Ta-da-da!

The York Road ended at the Elizabethtown Ferry and John Watson brought the Flying Machine to a screeching halt. He pulled a gold watch from his vest pocket to check the time. It was exactly three thirty. He smiled with satisfaction—the coach was right on schedule!

Before them lay the expanse of Newark Bay. The September sun shimmered on the water's surface while, overhead, seagulls glided in the breeze.

"This is the end of the road, ladies and gentlemen," John Watson announced as he helped his passengers from the coach. "I hope you enjoyed your trip on the Flying Machine!"

"A trifle too bumpy, Captain!" Miss Ruth remarked as she grasped his outstretched hand.

"It's no wonder they call these coaches 'spankers'!" Miss Martha interjected.

With his passengers and their luggage safely delivered, John Watson turned to David.

"Here's a present for you, lad," he said, handing him a copper coin. "It's not much but it will buy you an apple or a sweet cake. You were a good and helpful lad during the trip!"

David was overcome. "Oh, thank you, sir!" he said. "I enjoyed helping you, and, when I grow up I want to be a coachman just like you!"

John Watson threw his arm around the boy's shoulder and smiled.

The Elizabethtown Ferry was a sail ferry. As New York was twelve miles away across inland ocean waterways, the ferry required sails to move it along. It had to navigate through deep and difficult waters.

The passengers boarded the boat by means of a long wooden gangplank. On board there was much noise and bustle. The deck was full of ropes and hurrying sailors. A whistle blew and the gangplank was pulled in. The ferry was released from its moorings and drifted slowly into the bay. Within minutes its sails caught the wind.

David and the others waved good-bye to John Watson who remained on shore. He would wait there for the ferry to return from New York the following day. Then he would make the trip back to Philadelphia with new passengers. And when the time came for David to return home, he would be greeted by the familiar figure of John Watson waiting by his Flying Machine.

The big square sails billowed in the breeze and moved the ferry swiftly down the bay into the Kill Van Kull. This waterway connects Newark Bay with New York Bay.

The ferry rolled and pitched as it moved along and the water slapped noisily against its wooden sides.

Along the way, the shores on either side were heavily wooded. Here and there appeared the occasional outline of a house or a small village. In the distance, David saw thin lines of smoke rise from the chimneys of houses on Staten Island.

NEW YORK IN 1776

Once in the upper part of New York Bay, the ferry
passed several ocean-going vessels. One was the frigate,
"The Duchess of Somerset," and another, the brig,
"Friendship." It was exciting to watch the big ships sail by
and hear the sailors call out to each other as they passed.

In 1774, New York, although smaller than either Philadelphia or Boston, was an important colonial city. Its deep
natural harbor made it an excellent port and a center for
trade and commerce.

The sun was setting as the ferry reached the tip of Man-
hattan Island and entered the East River.

The city of New York stretched out before them as far

north as Chambers Street. Beyond that were farms and villages along Bloomingdale Road, now known as Broadway. David could see the tall stone warehouses rising above the wharves and the rows of quaint Dutch buildings with their stepped gable ends. The spire of Trinity Church was silhouetted against the sky and the windows of Fraunces Tavern were already ablaze with light.

In the distance, the British flag flapped in the breeze over the bastions of Fort George. The fort boasted a grand battery of twenty-three guns and a statue of its namesake, the English King, George III.

The ferry docked at the foot of Broad Street. Though

late in the day, the city still teemed with busy people. There were merchants checking cargo, stevedores tugging at heavy crates, Dutch farmers on their way home from market, shouting sailors and sea captains. The cobblestone streets were noisy with carriages and wagons.

In the midst of the crowd, David recognized the familiar faces of his aunt and uncle. They had come to meet him. He waved to them and, seeing him on board, they waved back.

He bid good-bye to Miss Martha, Miss Ruth, and Mr. Jeffers. Then, clutching the wooden hatbox, he stepped on shore. He was in New York. In two days he had traveled a little more than one hundred miles—through two colonies; across the Delaware; across the inland waters of the Atlantic. His journey on The York Road was over.

FOOT OF WALL STREET AND FERRY-HOUSE, 1746

Bibliography

CAWLEY, JAMES AND MARGARET. *Along the Old York Road.*
New Brunswick: Rutgers University Press, 1965.

EARLE, ALICE MORSE. *Stagecoach and Tavern Days.*
New York: Macmillan Co., 1902.

HOTCHKIN, S. F. *York Road, Old and New.*
Philadelphia: Binder and Kelly, 1892.

HONEYMAN, ROBERT. *Colonial Panorama 1775.* Edited by Philip Padelford.
San Marino: Huntington Library, 1936.

McROBERT, PATRICK. *A Tour Thru Part of the North Provinces of North America; Being a Series of Letters Wrote on the Spot in the Years 1774 and 1775.*
Edinburgh: 1776. Reprint. Philadelphia: Historical Society of Pennsylvania, 1935.

VAN SICKLE, EMOGENE. *Old York Road and Its Stagecoach Days.*
Copyright Emogene Van Sickle, 1937.

WILDES, HARRY EMERSON. *The Delaware.* Rivers of America Series.
New York: Rinehart and Company, 1940.

Coaching Terms

Box—high seat in front of the coach for the driver

Boots—deep luggage carriers at the front and rear of stagecoaches

Coach-and-four—a coach with four horses

Coacher—1: a coachman   2: a coach horse

Coach horn—a long straight tapering copper or brass horn with a slight flare

Coach horse—a horse used for pulling coaches, being heavier and of more compact build than a road horse

Coach house—an outbuilding for storage of a coach

Coachwhip—a whip with a long lash used in driving a coach

Concord stage—a coach suspended on two thick straps of leather called thoroughbraces. These caused the coach to sway and made the ride smoother. Concords were not made until 1826.

Ostler—a variation of hostler. One who takes care of horses at an inn.